How to Survive Sexuality as a Single Christian in a Sexually Driven Society

Introduction

As I am writing this, I am 12 days past my 50th Birthday. That's right, I'm a 50 Year Old Virgin! God has carried me through being laid off from jobs, relocating from my place or origin (Northern California) and has given me the blessing of traveling to other countries which I never knew I would go to due to coming from a Single-Parent, Middle Class home. PRAISE GOD!

Surviving Singleness

"Cosmopolitan" magazine, shows such as "Sex in the City" and other popular shows all point to what's called a "sex life" for the average adult (single adult that is...) in America. If you look at the present philosophy on sex in the world, none of it resembles the Bible at all. Condoms are given out in schools, local agencies can give a minor an abortion without Parental consent. How can a saved, blood-bought, born again, single christian stay obediently, celibate in today's society. Well, it's not easy, but it has and can be done ONLY BY THE HELP OF GOD! I will share and tell my journey and several others of how God has kept us in sexual purity (notice I say, GOD has kept us, and not US).

My Decision, The Decision

It was the early 80's and I was in my teems. My generation was the one after the Civil Rights movement because I was born towards the end of the movement. I was born in 1965, ten years after Dr. Martin Luther King and Rosa Parks started the movement in 1955. When I was in Elementary School, K-2nd grade, African Americans graduated from the terms of "Negro and Colored" to "Black" and "African American". There were "dashiki's", Afro's and Name-changing parties, and Black folks were coming into who they were. Even the television prime-time landscape was changing with shows such as "Julia", "The Jefferson's", "Sanford & Son", "That's My Mama", "Good Times" and others. There was a Sexual revolution as well; a Cultural revolution that still has its lingering affects.

The explicitness of sexual acts on R&B songs and disco's top 10 list left nothing to the imagination. Therefore, when I grew up, I already had the mindset of "having the right to Sexual freedom" or what the Bible would call "Sexual Bondage". So naturally, when I came to Christ at the age of 16, I made a vow to give away my Virginity at the age of 18. Whomever was to approach me at that time would be the "first taker", was going to have the privilege of being the "first". However, there was a DIVINE INTERVENTION in a youth Bible Study. Thank God for divine intervention of the Word stating no sex before marriage. When receiving the word, believe me, I didn't take it to heart right away. I argued and tried to justify my reasoning of my previous age sexual emancipation of "18". It took a bad experience, like most of us, to convince me of abstinence and celibacy.

During this time, I went on a date. The date didn't go well . It started with my date not having enough money to pay for the movie and me having to "pick up the slack". Then my date, truthfully, reminded me on how "hard I was on myself" and to work on my low self-esteem. We didn't "gel" well; I had misconceptions and I may have disappointed him. From this time forth, I said, LORD I SURRENDER MY DATING LIFE OVER TO YOU. This decision changed everything drastically.

My Change, My Repentance

Yes, I told the Lord to take over my dating life as you can tell. I was pursued and "hit on" by lots of guys at this time. Men of all ages, race and sizes showed me attention, so much so that I had "the talk" with my father and my mother. Men were approaching me. Also within this time frame, I learned about another important aspect with Single Christianity. I learned that "God wants us to date people who are like us" according to II Cor 6:14. So this narrowed down half of the population or ¾ of population that were coming after me. So, the prospects slowed down and dried up. The strange phenomenon of less men came about in my life. I was interested in Christ a lot more and was undergoing a great change in my life which took place from the heart! I was on my way to being a mature single christian, who was sold out for the LORD. It didn't mean the desires went away; believe me, they were still there.

During this growth and according to Scripture, we are owned by God (I Cor 6-12-18). Property, ownership and belongings are terms used or inanimate objects and are usually not associated with human beings. We are free, individual humans who are created different but, we are equal according to our Constitution (developed by our "Founding Fathers"). However, when we give our lives to Christ, this philosophy goes out of the window. We become "God's Property" and are no longer our own. We belong to God, and according to the Word of God, we are his children, his bride and his church. Well, if you think of the early church and how it was referred to as "the church", which is synonymous with the "temple".

The "temple" was a place of worship and was constructed to detail in the old testament in books such as Exodus, Leviticus and II Chronicles. Solomon, David and Bathsheba son, had the detailed task of, building the Temple of God. The temple is where worship took place and very specific vessels were used as a part of the service. There was the Outer court, the Holy place, the Lamp stand, and eventually the Holiest of Hollies. After the dispensation of grace, we have become the temple of God. As God would dwell in the temple or tabernacle of the Old Testament, He dwells in us. Unlike the Old Testament, the Spirit of God doesn't go and come in us. His presence is constant. However, in order for Gods' presence to remain the temple, the temple must be in exact order as instructed by God and remember God is holy, which means, it must be clean and undefiled. Well, just as the temple of the old testament had to be clean and undefiled we are to be also. We belong to God and are redeemed and are a "peculiar" people. We are in no way "common" or "ordinary". My change took place when I surrendered fully to God in this area and as I became in love with him, I wanted to please him more. This desire and a set of circumstances caused the change within me.

Christ's Purchase (I Cor 6:12-20)

While on the journey before the construction of the temple, the Lord dwelled in the tabernacle which was a picture or an early version of the temple. God dwelled in the temple in order to guide the children of Israel on the next place of instruction. However, his indwelling of the tabernacle or his presence really symbolized his mastery or his owning and protection of his children or "his property". We, according to I Cor. 6:12-20, we are his property. He will guide you, protect you, but most importantly, he owns you as a "blood bought, blood washed" believer. He indwells the Single Christian to show his mastery and care. The love and purchase was shown on Calvary. The mastery is shown in the indwelling of the Holy Spirit. Remember, in order for God or the Holy Spirit to indwell and rule, we must not allow any defilement to come in. This alone is the real reason and case against fornication and the charge to the Single Christian.

In the New Testament book of I Corinthians, the Corinthians had certain worship practices that Paul had to correct them on. One of the practices involved sexual acts as a part of worship. I Corinthians 6:19-22 tells us that we are to keep the temple undefiled by not engaging in fornication and that fornication is the only sin that is "against the body". Other sins are birthed within or are started in the mind. Fornication, although through lust within, is the only sin against the body because you join your body with someone in union and a soul is or will be tied to each other. That person is basically taking the place of God or some other entity is. This scripture shows that we are the temple and a great investment was made for us by the Jesus the Son of God and to be a dwelling place for the Holy Spirit.

Pictures Of Fornication

God is a relational God, meaning he loves relationships. He is a monogamous lover and wants all to him no open relationships with him. We are the "bride of Christ" according to scripture, meaning he is the groom. We are cleaned, bought with a price and are to be without spot or blemish. We are seen as a "bride" to be ready for him. When you are at the engagement stage of a relationship, there is one word to explain the relationship at this stage and that is "exclusivity". You are sole property and your mate has exclusive right to you entirely and vice verse. When you give yourself to someone in fornication, you breach a contract or covenant. God seems to lose his property, but most unfortunately, the intimacy is lost. In books such as Isaiah, Jeremiah and Ezekiel, the children of Israel had a cycle of for disobedience and then obedience.

God symbolizes or makes the analogy of idolatry to fornication or "lifting the dress" and "sharing nakedness". Fornication is a form of betrayal and brings pain and ruptures intimacy. In these pictures of fornication, Israel has committed a sin, either by not obeying God or mostly commonly committed Idolatry. This always results in alienation from the Lord because he is a God who wants full devotion to himself. There is a break in their relationship with God. In the same way, when fornication is committed, you defile the temple and you are joining your soul to someone.

When you are not married and have sex outside of marriage, your body joins itself to someone you are not committed to and a "soul tie" is created. With soul ties, you make that person to be a part of your Spiritual life. I have spoken with married couples who normally have sexual relations as married couples are supposed to. It is common that one spouse can literally "feel" when the person is upset without even asking them if they are. They can sense when their spouse is in trouble and can feel others things due to their "souls" being tied with each other. Sex is a privilege of marriage because of this reason. This is the way its supposed to be with married couples and remember, the picture of our relationship is a picture of marriage with God. When listening to Married couples, sex is the "icing on the cake" and is the factor of intimacy in marriage. By sexual intercourse, they are closest as two people can get and showing the highest level of intimacy. In I Corinthians chapter 6, it reiterates that we as Single people are to solely have intimacy with God and not "share our soul" with anyone who does not have exclusive right of a spouse with us. God wants to be intimate with us. Fornication, being the only sin against the body, doesn't allow intimacy with God. Our souls at this point, is "tied" with someone else and the temple is defiled and the Holy Spirit cant really dwell freely in a defiled temple. Don't get me wrong; there is a such thing as "repentance", reformation and revival. None of us are perfect. However, I am referring to a "lifestyle" that the world seems to approve of which is referred to as being "sexually active". Fornication doesn't really allow intimacy with God.

Pictures of Purity

If you have read the word of God and been a Christian as long as I have, you've noticed that God is referred to as light, holy and most of all is synonymous with purity. When he dwells within or interact with someone or something, it is either one of two things: the first and only of its kind, and is clean and pure. Does this mean that Singles have to be perfect and pure? When it comes to perfection, by all means no. When studying the scriptures, perfection is not defined as "without flaw" it usually means "maturity". When the word "purity" is used, it usually means "set apart" meaning exclusivity.

This definition is one of the definitions for the word "holy". Being set a part doesn't mean perfection but "uniqueness" or something used for a specific reason. It denotes we are exclusive to God. God wants all of us and full devotion! You think about and consider this. Remember your first "crush" or your first "love"? This person was constantly on your mind. Your heart "skipped a beat" when in their presence and they had your full attention. If you're a female like me, you waited by the phone for their call. You were, whether you realize it or not, devoted to them. When your relationship gets physical, devotion more than likely switches to that person and not to God.

The idea of purity is being undefiled or unalloyed. When walking with the Lord, God is attracted to full devotion, and purity in regards to sexual activity (or no sexual activity). Since he is holy,he relates to the clean and those things set apart. We are set apart as vessels to bring other Singles and the like to Christ. If we are like them, what can we use to attract them?

So Why Does the Devil Want You to Lose your Virginity and not

Endure

Remember, our bodies are the "temple of the Holy Spirit". If we defile it by fornication, the Master of the throne is no longer master. The Devil has always been in competition with God over who is ruler over temporal things. When fornication is present the soul is joined with whomever you sleep with and God is no longer "king". Satan wants us to be defiled. The enemy knew, in the Garden of Eden, that he could get Adam & Eve to disobey God. The relationship with him could suffer and God would not be Lord and there would be a separation. The enemy has always been jealous of man's position or creation. God gave Adam lordship of creation and this was the original position of Lucifer but he blew it. We all know that the enemy (Lucifer or Satan) will go to hell and be in the "lake of fire". He wants others to be separate from God and join him in his final destination. He has also wanted to master over mankind. In order to do this, he must separate mankind from God, and one of the ways to separate the Single Christian from fellowship with God is by illicit sex and fornication. If you look at the things that plague cities like Corinth and such; you will see that they used sex or rituals that involved sexual intercourse as a part of their religion. The sexual act, as state earlier, is a joining of the body and the soul. It's also has a connotation of mastery, and as we all know, there can only be one master! Whenever you obey God, he is master.

Why Sex is for Married People

One might ask, "Why are married people only entitled to sex?" After studying and reviewing a few things, I found several reasons why they are privileged to this act. Married people are to have sex for the following reasons: Procreation, Intimacy and "oneness" which is God's will.

Procreation

If you remember, in Genesis, God commanded the birth and creation of mankind by saying "be fruitful and multiply". God wants us to have children and other generations, a Godly lineage and in order to do this sexual intercourse has to take place. However, according to God's word the context of sexual intercourse has a specific place. In the mid to late eighties, there was the idea of "test tube" babies. These were babies created from female and male reproductive properties taken outside the body and then fertilized in a laboratory within a test tube. In the millennium, there is the study "cloning". This is obviously not God's way. Children should be the natural result of a marriage. Creation is something God intended from the start and he enabled his creatures, mankind, with the ability to procreate out of love. If you have ever taken Biology or any science class, you were probably taught about Amoeba's. Amoebas are one of few creatures that procreate a-sexually (meaning without intercourse. Animals,although male & female reproduce when urges hit them and when the female is "in heat". We can procreate similarly like animals, but ideally, married people can make love or create out of intimacy and love.

Intimacy and Oneness

If you look at the physical aspect of sexual intercourse, the man and the woman are as close as two people can get. They are intimate. Sex is exclusive to married people because it is a picture and act of intimacy. Ideally in obedience to God, they are exclusive to each other and only their spouse has the privilege of making love or sexual intercourse with them and NO ONE ELSE has the right except their spouse. They share this beautiful act only with each other and with no one else. It is the exclusive right of their spouse. The exclusivity of it shows intimacy. If you think about our relationship with God, through Christ, we share things with God that we do not share with others, the sexual act should be shared only with your spouse.

Intimacy of sex is for the married to being closeness and also fulfills another part of marriage that God wants and that is oneness. God said in Genesis, "for this reason, a man shall leave his Mother and

Father and cleave to his wife". Most importantly, it says, "and the two shall become one". In marriage, the wife and husband become as one body. This is why when divorce happens, they say it's like "ripping" yourself in half because at one point (consummation of marriage) there was once oneness. God allows intercourse because it is a symbol of oneness. When the act happens, it shows intimacy like stated previously. Married people have the right to join themselves to each other, in essence, becoming "one body". This, I believe, is why sex is allowed in marriage. Oneness is the goal of marriage and shows God's intention of marriage. God developed two people in the beginning stating that man should not be alone, so he created, woman the "helper suitable" for Adam. God's will was or started with two people who were the first married couple on the earth. God's will is for marriage intimacy through sexual intercourse. In Genesis, God commanded for Adam and Eve to be fruitful and multiply.

The Bride or Christ: God's Relationship with Us

God is not a stranger to relationships, love and sex. After all, he created all three. Haven't you noticed that in the book of Revelation, we as the body of Christ, are seen as the "bride of Christ" He, Jesus is the "bridegroom". Isn't it strange that the symbols, analogies or pictures of our relationship with God is "marriage" or as "newlyweds". We are married to God and are to be intimate with God. Our relationship with God is not only as "Father and Child" but as spouses who are intimate. We are to be sold out and exclusive with each other. We are set apart, holy, if you will, to God. If you think about a marriage, what should be the center of all marriages? There is a four-letter word and that is LOVE (L-O-V-E). God's love is also shown by being a bridegroom or husbandman to us.

In the Gospel of John, it starts out stating that we are the vine and my father is the vine dresser or as King James says, the "husbandman". This is an old term or vine dressers or those who take care of the vines. A husbandman takes care of his crop, vines or what is his. Now, as you will read in chapter 15 of the Gospel of John, we are the vines, Jesus is the vine and God is the vine dresser or husbandman. We are to stay connected to the Vine in order to be taken care of by the vine dresser or husbandman. I like to think of it as we have a way through our Lord and Savior Jesus Christ as being intimate with the husbandman.

Do you notice how lovingly the vine dresser or husbandman pays a lot of attention to the vine. If you ever study this chapter, he takes great care of the branches because with the branches. The vine is highly important but if there are not branches to the vine, which produces fruit, there is no reason for the vine to exist. God prunes and wants to be intimate with us for his sake. It says in verse 8 of that same chapter that "it glorifies God that we bare much fruit".

Fornication in the singles life stagnates or hinders fruit from growing. Fruit in the singles life is freedom, intimacy with God and blessings that he wants to give us. When unbelieving single see a Christian single who is not constantly trying to "pick up" the opposite sex at the bars, or who is happy and content without constantly being in emotional draining relationships, this saved single is showing fruit. It causes the unbelieving single to ask, "how do you live without someone in your life?". Little do they know, you do have someone in your life and that is Christ. Your abstinence and celibacy adds more "weight" when you testify about Christ in your life. Your abstinence, celibacy and "sexual purity" serves as "fruit" you are bearing which glorifies God. Just as a good marriage has the "perk" of sexual intercourse and show love to each other, God wants intimacy with the saved single and will shower love on them.

How Do You Do It or Not Do It?

So, you might ask, "how do you do it?". How do you stay celibate in this sexual driven society? Well, in order for me to address this, I have to get back in my "Delorean Time machine" and go back toe the mid to late 80's. I was a late-teen or young adult during this time. I was hungry for God being a new believer and was attending a Bible study for Youth at the church I was attending at the time. We were taught the word about Fornication and what it meant. We were also taught about being "unequally yoked with unbelievers" as mentioned in II Corinthians. This takes us back to the date I previously mentioned. I had a date with an unbeliever that coming weekend. The date was a disaster. I was self conscientious and critical which as out of nervousness and a "turn off" to my date. He was a guy who did not have enough money for the movie, we didn't see eye to eye or really get along.

During the date, we did not have good conversations when "getting to know" each other. Also, when questioned, he was not a believer. However, I felt a sexual overtone about him and he expected a kiss good night. Although I was corrected about my self image and we didn't get along, I made a special prayer after that date. I prayed and said "Lord, from this time on, I give you full permission to take over my date life and allow you to choose a mate for me, when you want and in whatever way you want". At this time, having a future mate was not really on the forefront of my mind due to being under the age of 30. However, I was trying to not fall into fornication. This is why I prayed the prayer that I did. I was so convicted by the Word of God that I wanted to please him in this area.

God used this situation to open up my spiritual eyes. It brought about humility. Humility as in the same way that Solomon had when he asked God for wisdom in I Kings and II Chronicles chapter 1. I was forced to "surrender" this area of my life over to God, which was the key. It was not my self-will, or that I made up my mind. Let's face it, we all have the same flesh, the same hormones and the same tendencies. I Corinthians 10:12 says "Let him who thinks he stands take heed lest he fall..", and then it goes into the great verse we all use for "temptation", I Corinthians 10:13. You must surrender your sexual life or what the world calls "sexuality" to God.

Sexuality for the Save Single is nothing other than celibacy and abstinence. You basically don't do or not do anything but SURRENDER to God and let God do it through you. You may have heard of many people who were delivered from anger, pain, drug use and yes fornication and adultery. There is something about falling in love with Jesus and wanting to please him and surrender to Him totally. He changes your want and desires and your focus. You begin to read, digest and "eat" the Word of God. You spend hours in the word and prayer. You will have "worship sessions" on your own and then the next thing you know, one year goes by with you being sexually pure. The next year goes by, and other years past. What normally happens to people (I have witnessed it), God arranges and give "divine appointment" where you meet your husband or wife and then there is a marriage and consummation takes place.

During the years of abstinence and celibacy, you will give an "aurora" of Christ which means you wont have non-Christians "hitting on you". Strange guys will not try to "pick you up" due to you being in a circle of people who have the same goal as you and that is to please God. Your Spirit filled life will serve as protection for you. You change and Romans 12:1-2 will happen to you, "being transformed by the renewing of your mind".

Falling in Love with Jesus and Yourself

While getting into the Word, walking with Christ you will start to develop a relationship. It's like your dating someone. When I was new to Christ and decide to give my dating life or "sexuality" to God, I surprised those who were close to me. Like most believers, I ate, slept and drank Jesus. I became fanatic for sure. I even had a bumper sticker on the back of my old Plymouth that said "Jesus is the Reason for My Life". You see, I was in love with Jesus but still had to learn to love one more person, and that was myself. As the years have gone by, I learned to love me because Christ loves me. I finally learned that I am "fearfully and wonderfully made" according to Psalm 139. God loved me better than I loved myself. It is known spiritually and securely that in order for someone else to love you, you must love yourself. In scripture, Gods love for us is noted throughout the Bible. He will love me no matter what.

I believe that God gives some of us time in this area in order for us to be all that we can be for our future mates. When there is low self-esteem and insecurity, it makes it impossible for a marriage to work (I have been on a date with a Christian guy who's marriage was destroyed because of this fact).

Get Ready for Ridicule and a Lot of Questions

According to the World, singles are adults, who should be dating and "playing the field", using contraceptives having a "healthy sexual life". However, after they encounter you, a Single Christian who does "swap" a lot of stories about the opposite sex. People notice something different about you. You don't "kiss and tell" or talk about "exchanging keys" to your partners apartment. You are cool, calm and collected. They don't see you with the opposite sex as much as other single people. They say things like, "how come your not married?", or "when are we going to hear the pitter-patter of little feet around your home" (for those of us who don't have any children) or they may ask "you don't have any kids?, Why?".

These type of questions are what you will hear and may come across as ridicule in a way. You will see people, who are your age, have date after date and a few children. The enemy and others may start to "mess with your mind" and make you feel like your missing something or that life is passing you by. On the contrary, you have the way, the truth and the life. Although the statistics have decreased, there still are a number of heterosexuals as well as homosexuals who contract the aids virus. Timing in the Kingdom of God is very important. You will be a fish swimming upstream, going against the tide. However, you must remember that according to I Peter, we are a "peculiar people" and this world is not our home.

When you feel left out and lonely, do what I do, think of Hannah, mother of Samuel. If you read I Samuel and read about and

Penninah and Hannah, the two wives of Elkanah the priest. Penninah was the wife that gave birth to several children, while Hannah appeared barren. She was not able to give birth to a child up to this point. During these times, it was a disgrace for a wife not give birth to a child or be barren. I identify with Hannah. She had to watch Penninah give birth time after time with pain and weeping, wishing she could so "bless" Elkanah. However, she called out to God with her hearts desire, even promising God that if she was blessed with a son, she would dedicate him right back to Him.

After a period of time, God acted in loving kindness like he normally does and heard her prayer, opened her womb and gave birth to Samuel. She honored her promise and dedicated Samuel to him. The reason for me giving this analogy is that you will be the opposite of the norm and there may be a long span of singleness for you as a Christian. What we can always count on is the fact that God loves, cares about us and wants to best for us. He hears our cry and wants our loneliness to be a void that points us to him. Remember, this same Samuel later grew up to be a judge and witnessed the children of Israel appoint themselves a King which was against God's word. Saul was appointed as King and messed when he brought back spoils from a war in which God had instructed of all of these particular people

Samuel had to give him the word that stated, "rebellion is as the sin of witchcraft" and that "obedience is better than sacrifice".

Obedience, which includes abstaining from fornication, will be better than compromise and sacrifice. It can be done by surrendering to God and the power of the Holy Spirit. Just think, you are the opposite of the world and the first thing that will come out of their mouth is "why?" or questioning whether you are hetero or homosexual. You have to remember, or ask yourself "If I were to compromise, will these people be there when my heart is broken and pick up the pieces of my testimony and life after I have a one-night stand?" You are God's child and remember, "rebellion is as the sin of witchcraft."

The one thing that will keep us on track and pure is the Word of God. When you surround yourself with other saints, especially single saints, you are less likely to focus on the ridicule and off comments from others. The one thing I used to say to myself is "I need another addictive sin like I need another hole in my head". Stay in the Word of God and remind yourself of the scriptures that focus on fleeing fornication and sexual immorality. Be encouraged by Joseph and other who obeyed God and were blessed. Don't be hurt or offended by others.

Obey the Word of God. There have been times where I disobeyed the promptings of the Holy Spirit (non sexual of course) and have lost out on certain blessings. There is nothing worst than realizing that you have disobeyed and hurt God. Getting into the Word of God will cause you to fall in love with him and not want to hurt him in any way, even sexually.

The Single Mind and Single-mindedness

If you haven't learned by now, when you are not married, you are what we call "Single". When you are single, we tend to think that God is far from us. It is important to know what God says to Singles. God loves the unmarried just as much as the married. This information is shown in I Corinthians. The Corinthians were heavily involved in pagan worship which involved "Temple Prostitutes". Therefore he had to write and make things clear in regards to Singles.

As unmarried people, we are: free to serve God, responsible to God only, More able to have and be used of in ministries, and are loved God as well. We are not less important, Awkward, or anything of the sort You will want to be Holy as he is Holy. However Holiness doesn't mean perfect.

What Holiness Means

God not only calls Married children of God to be Holy, but Singles are to be Holy. If you study or look at the vessels used in the Temple of God for the tabernacle of the Old testament, there were certain parts for certain practices. This vessel was set a part for a certain task. The vessel is "holy" for a certain reason. We as Singles are holy for certain task. Our holiness for singles is to reflect the Love of Christ to the world. When you are set a part or holy, you behave and function in a certain way by the power of the Holy Spirit. Knowing this, you as a Single child of God, do not act a certain way because of who you belong to.

Holiness is not perfection. It is not wearing fully concealed outfits (remember, God loves a sinner with a low-cut, V-neck blouse who has surrendered to Christ rather than a conservatively, proud and self-righteous judgmental saint any day). Holiness is , you not drinking "soft-drinks" only or seeing "PG-13" movies exclusively. It is a surrendered heart to God and loving him so much that you want to please him in every way. At this point, you realize that you can only live the Christian life by the Holy Spirit. Holiness is saying, "God I trust you to help me be the single you want me to be, change me so that I don't fornicate." Holiness is realizing that when you fall, you don't beat yourself up. Holiness is not judging others. Holiness is walking with God and before you know it reflect attributes of your Father in Heaven.

Importance of Obedience

Holiness makes your usable to God. When you do this, you are obeying God. There are two things that show God that we love and trust him and that is faith and obedience. This surrendering is what has kept me from fornication from the age of 18. In order to please God, we must obey him and that includes ALL areas of life not just in the area of fornication. Obedience is required in the Single person's life as well as the Married person. Obedience is important because it shows God we are not our own and we love him. Obedience is important for your basic necessities in life and well being. Obedience is important due to God blessings for us, and is most important due to us showing that we are children of the "Most High" and makes us more attractive to others. It makes us "salty" to the world. Obedience is the "litmus test" that shows whether we love God and trust him or don't. Be Abraham and believe and obey without question.

So Can Christian Singles Date?

The answer to the above question is yes. However, if you read II Corinthians 6:14, we are to date each other. We are to date believers who love God like we do. There are also different focuses on Christian dating or what is called "courtship". Courtship is a lost word in our society. Only in old movie or times past do you hear the word "courting". Dating is the newer term and was not used in previous generations. It came about at the end of the 20th century. This is when society and women's liberation was coming to the main stream of our society. Courtship existed before this. After studying several books by Christian authors and therapist, "dating" is associated with "short-term" or temporary relationships, while "courtship" focuses on a long-term relationship progressing to marriage.

Parents are involved in courtship and the "touching" or "kissing" part comes later in the courtship. If you think about dating, this touching or kissing part usually starts in the beginning of the relationship. In courtship, you are allowed to really get to know the person. You discover each others character, ways, likes and dislikes. Saying this, most Christians point toward courtship (or should) over dating. Christians, Single Christians are allowed to meet and have romance and love and courtship but in accordance to I Corinthians 6 and II Corinthians 6:14 and the word of God.

Being extraordinary instead of "sex-traordinary" is our goal. When you think of the word "extraordinary", you know its something, uncommon, special and its stands out from the "norm". When you are not a sexually active single, your are in a different category. You don't meet the definition of a single person in the world and automatically have a life that "mirrors" Christ. Sex isn't the main focus of your life and allows you to be solely devoted to God. Remember that when someone gives themselves sexually, they give their soul away or "tie" their soul to that person.

Ephesians says that fornication is the only sin that is committed against the body. When you do this, your souls is not fully God's and the other person shares the throne with God. God wants all of us as Singles. Our lives and souls are fully his. At point, we are not joined our body with anyone. We are one by ourselves, unlike our Married brothers and sisters who must join and be "one". Their souls should be "tied" to each other as one and their joined soul belongs to God. With singles, your soul is tied to God only.

What if I Messed Up?

A lot of you know the world we live in and you may ask, "what if you lost your virginity already?" or even worst, someone may have taken your virginity by molestation or rape. The word of God says, "if any man be in Christ Jesus, he is a new creature". When you give your life to Christ, your sins are washed away and the healing of the past can begin as soon as you to the "s" word, and that is SURRENDER to God. At this moment, you are what I call a "new" or "regenerated" virgin. Remember the word "new". God wants us to grow in him and surrender to him so that we can live the life he wants by his power. What he told the woman who was caught in adultery was to "go and sin no more". To God, he is always concerned about a life of obedience, walking and trusting him on a moment by moment basis. When anyone gives their life to Christ, the Holy Spirit enables us to live a life that pleases God, including being abstinent.

If you had a life of fornication, you can do all things through Christ who strengthens you. Although I am a virgin in this state of my life, my heart goes out to people who are caught up in this lifestyle. You may ask, "how do you know God can keep you after living a life of fornication when you have never had a sexual encounter?" Being a Christian for so long has caused me to observe a lot of people and have heard a lot of testimonies. I have seen adults who were not only used sex to get what they want and have several children out of wedlock give testimonies of a life of sexual purity, but I have seen people who were Heroin addicts, and whore mongers simultaneously be freed from both vices only by the power of the Holy Spirit. You must remember, Paul was a Pharisee circumcised on the 8th day and breathed threats against Christians. After his conversion on the road to Damascus, he became a Christian who loved Christ, he also was the first Missionary for Christ and ended writing up to 2/3rds of New Testament. Our God can keep and change anyone.

Virginity into Adulthood

During this time, you must realize you will have certain practices down and be strong in other areas. However, you must remember that the same way the Lord has kept you since salvation, is the same Holy Spirit that will continue to keep you into adulthood. On the other had, just as David fell in one moment, so can you.

You will have to focus on Christ and have a resolve to obey in all areas including sexual purity. If you have to not watch some of the most popular TV shows due to where it takes you "mentally", then don't watch it. If you go on a date and if walking you to your front door for a "good night kiss will lead you to a passionate moment, then don't do it. There is always blessings in being obedient to God. We want to please Him, and make it so that our potential mates will be able to have the great prize at our weddings, our purity and virginity. I am speaking to all Single Christians, male and female alike. Make it your goal to please God in every way.

So, What are the Actual Steps to Surviving Sexually as a Single Christian?

By this time, you may be asking, "what steps can I do to stay away from fornication literally?" Well, I'm glad you asked. I have covered why you must abstain from fornication, now I'm going to some practical steps as to how you, by the power of the Holy Spirit, can deter sexual immorality:

Step 1: Surrender your Dating/Courting Life to God and Repent of any areas of Fornication and Sexual Immorality. Surrendering to this area of your life to God is what I've been saying all along, I'm now going to tell you how to do this practically.

A) Repent and tell the Lord, "God, I confess and admit that I have a problem with Sexual immorality and Fornication, I want to obey you in this area and ask for forgiveness and cleansing of this sin. I can only do this through you and need your help with staying Sexually pure and abstaining from Fornication. Lord I surrender this area over to you and make a commitment to obey you through the power of the Holy Spirit. I allow you to choose my mate for me and I will abstain from Sexual intercourse until my Wedding night by your grace."

B) If you haven't fallen in this area but have been tempted or simply haven't thought much about it, you can surrender by praying,

"Father, I want to please you in all areas in my life including the area of Sexual immorality. From this moment on, I surrender my Dating/Courting area of my life over to you. I resolve to be obedient to you and will abstain from Sex before Marriage by the power of the Holy Spirit. I allow you to choose my mate for me and I will abstain from Sexual intercourse until my Wedding night by your grace."

Your humility by repentance or surrendering is the first step. When we humble ourselves, we allow God to restructure us and we are walking in the Spirit. This is communion, dependence and obedience to God. Dependence on the Father, Son and Holy Spirit is key to living the Christian Life.

Step 2: Study and Note Scriptures and Verses on Fornication and Sexual Immorality

If you read Matthew 4, you will read the account of Jesus being led in the wilderness to be tempted. Jesus fought the Devil by using scripture. All three attempts were defeated by Him quoting the Word of God. This is your "sword" in the Armor of God. You must know the Word in order to be victorious. When you are tempted, use the Word of God, not just in this area, but in all areas of your life.

Step 3: Surround Yourself with other Single Christians who are OBEDIENT in this area and are Sexually pure:

Psalm 1 says "Blessed is the man who walketh not in the counsel of the ungodly..." As you know, when the word often uses "man" it mean "woman" as well. This means, you are to fellowship with people who have made a commitment to be obedient to God by not living a life of Fornication who are saving themselves for marriage (regardless of what their past is). Even if they have recently been delivered in this area. It says in I Corinthians 15:33 that "bad company corrupts good morals".

Step 4: When you Date, Date other Christians.

II Corinthians 6: 14-18 says that we are to date other people who are believers like we are ("For what right does darkness have to light or Christ with Belial..."). Dating and unbeliever will only complicate things. Although you may "get along", there will always be a "divide" in what you believe and most secular people are taught that sex outside of marriage is o.k as long as you are responsible (meaning the use of contraceptives). Although there are some "Carnal Christians" out there, if you tell your Christian date that you are being obedient to the Word of God, they should understand. If they don't, get out of the relationship.

Step 5: Minimize Time Spent Alone with Your Date.

The whole goal is for you to not make the mistake of getting in an environment conducive for a sexual act. Things such as inviting your date up for coffee after a date while you are a Single who lives alone with no roommates or sitting in a car at "Lookout Point" with the new girl who just joined Youth Group at 10PM on a Saturday night, may not be good ideas for Christian Singles to do. As a Warning, don't think that just because you are currently a virgin, that you can't suddenly find your self in a compromising situation. I have heard of a couple, who were both virgins, who spent a lot of time, alone together and they both fell into fornication with each other. I'm not saying to not spend time alone with your date at all. However, I am telling you to use caution and remember I Corinthians 10:12, "He who thinks s he stand let him take heed lest he fall..". Remember, these type of feelings aren't bad; it's just to be used in the context of marriage. God made sex and its to be used in the right place.

Step 6: Try to Abstain from Sexually Explicit Media

This may seem next to impossible in our society. However, you can do it, because God helps me to do it. I would suggest staying away from: Pornographic websites and other forms of media, TV shows, Music and Music Videos, Movies, Magazines and Books that are Sexually explicit or that go against what the Word of God says regarding Sexual immorality. In Matthew 6:22-23, is says that the Light of the body is the eye and how it is to be filled with "light". When you participate in any of these things, we are filling it with darkness. In I John 4 it states that God is light and in him there is no darkness. If he is light, we want to be filled with Him. Watching these type of subjects for a long period of time will only deter you from Sexual purity and lead to Fornication.

Step 7: Have an Intimate Relationship with God by Prayer, Fasting and Spending time with Him.

This is the most important step of all. This means walking with God. What is walking with God? It means to have communion, dependence and obedience with God. In communing with Him, you talk to him about EVERYTHING. In depending on God, you RELY ON HIM FOR EVERYTHING, ESPECIALLY ABSTINENCE. In obeying him, your goal is to OBEY AND DO EVERYTHING HE TELLS YOU TO DO. If you "mess up", there is I John 1:9, confess your sin, He will cleanse you from ALL unrighteousness. A good chapter to study is

Matthew Chapter 6. You discover Jesus' model of prayer for us amongst other things and most importantly it leads you to a verse you have probably heard quoted numerous times in Church. That verse is Matthew 6:33, "Seek ye first the Kingdom of God and his righteousness and all these things shall be added unto you". When you think of a "kingdom", it means that you are under the subjection to whomever is on the throne. You obey his laws of the land and are under his rule. With being in the Kingdom of God, you are to obey the Law of the Lord and you are under the rule of the "King of Kings".

My Challenge to You as a Single Christian

My challenge to all Single Christians is to live for Christ, Love Christ and the lead by Christ. Keep the same excitement and fervor that you had when you were a New Christan. When things like going to Church or Bible Study start to get "stale and mundane", go on a fast, pray and get in his presence by worship or just sitting quietly before him with no distractions. Your relationship with Jesus should be the most important thing in your life. It will rank higher than your future marriage and calls for you to be Sexually pure. Regardless of your background or if you have been recently delivered in this area, let nothing hinder your relationship with God. Let's all pray for each other as Singles, to stay obedient and surrendered to him sexually and keep ourselves until marriage. Let's all be intimate with Him shall we.